A Journey Toward HOPE

Written by **Victor Hinojosa** & **Coert Voorhees**
Illustrations by **Susan Guevara**

SIXFOOTPRESS
Houston

Ten-year-old Alessandra says goodbye to the rippling waters of Lake Petén Itzá, in Guatemala.

She tries to remember her mother, who left four years ago, hugging Alessandra close before she went, who promised to send for her as soon as there was money.

"I'm coming to meet you, Mamá," Alessandra says softly as she walks away from the water's edge.

Laura is thirteen and wants to go to school. Nando is seven and likes trains. They wish they could stay in El Salvador, but their parents want them to live with their aunt and uncle in the United States.

"I don't want to leave," Nando says through his tears.

"I'll be with you, Nando," Laura replies. "We can be strong together."

In San Pedro Sula, Honduras, fourteen-year-old Rodrigo's friends are doing things they shouldn't be doing. They want him to join them, but he refuses.

He kneels next to his sleeping little sister. If he tells her he is leaving, she will beg him to stay.

"I'm going to join our parents in Nebraska. Soon we will all be together and be happy." Rodrigo leaves the note on the pillow near her head and walks out of the house.

Rodrigo and Alessandra meet in El Ceibo as they are about to cross into Mexico.

"Ma sa' laach'ool," she says. "Good morning. Are you going to America?"

"Hello," Rodrigo answers. "I am. You, too?"

This girl with the colorful dress reminds Rodrigo of his sister. Alessandra can sense that this mop-haired boy with the tattered shoes is a good person.

Halfway across the Suchiate River, Laura slips on the edge of the raft and tumbles into the rushing water.

"Laura!" Nando screams, reaching for her fingertips. "Don't leave me!"

A stranger lifts her back into the boat, and Nando hugs her tight. They finally make it to dry land, exhausted. They are now in Mexico.

At a shelter in Oaxaca, the four children huddle on the same cardboard mattress. Even though they just met, they pass the night together like family.

Nando's belly growls. "Was that a jaguar?" Laura asks with a forced laugh.

"Yook intz'okajik," Alessandra says, rubbing her stomach.

Rodrigo nods. Everybody understands hunger. "We'll find something to eat soon. Tomorrow, we ride La Bestia, the train."

"Run and climb onto the train when it slows at the curve!"
Alessandra yells as La Bestia approaches.

Nando sprints with everything he has. He is the smallest,
but he is also the fastest. One day, he will be a track star.

As Rodrigo leaps for the iron ladder, his shoe tumbles down, sliced instantly in half by the wheels of the train. But he makes it on. They all do.

The children catch their breath, relieved for now, and find one another amid the crowds atop the boxcars.

"We are moving!" Laura yells. "Woohoo!"

The Throwers surprise them with bundles of bread, crackers, and bottles of water. They throw other things onto the train, too: a sweater, a doll, shoes.

Some of the Throwers have also sent their own children on the journey toward hope. They help these children now, praying that others will do the same for their kids.

Laura combines the Throwers' gifts to make a proper meal: bread, cheese, soda, lemonade. She will be a chef one day, just like her mother.

For one beautiful moment, the children feel strong again.

In Mexico City, the kids hop off the train and soon find themselves in the largest market they have ever seen. It's loud, a frenzy of color and energy and unfamiliar words.

Here, some people are kind. A woman gives Rodrigo a pair of shoes that fit his bare, blistered feet. Others give them a mango, a loaf of bread, a bar of soap.

The next day, the children climb back onto La Bestia. It is very crowded. They squeeze into whatever space they can find.

A man crawls along the top of a covered traincar. He fell down when the train moved suddenly, and his leg is bleeding. Rodrigo tears a strip off his shirt and wraps the wound. One day, he will be a doctor.

The train rattles through tunnels so long that the kids forget what light looks like. The Beast belches black smoke that clogs their noses and makes them cough.

Nando's voice cuts through the darkness. "It will be worth all of this, right?"

"What will?" Alessandra asks.

"The future? On the other side?" he replies.

"Of course, in America we will go to school and always have enough to eat. We will be with our families," Alessandra answers. They all want to believe her.

Even with the hail and rain, the heat of the day, the night's bitter chill, they feel free.

Free, if only for a moment. The wind in their hair. Their futures open in front of them.

The children have finally made it as far as La Bestia can take them, still many miles from the border between Mexico and the United States.

A man with warm eyes and a gentle voice gives them and others a ride in the back of his pickup truck.

As Rodrigo talks to the man through the window, Alessandra sees thousands of monarch butterflies migrating in the other direction.

She pictures infinity in her mind. She sees the history of her ancestors, the Mayans, and feels their strength flowing through her. She will become an artist.

At the Nuevo Laredo camp in Mexico, across the Rio Grande from Laredo, Texas, they gaze at the United States for the first time.

Tomorrow, they will cross the bridge and ask for asylum. The members of this new family formed during their journey will have to go their separate ways.

But that is tomorrow. Tonight, they dream.

Alessandra hums her mother's favorite song.

Nando and Laura snuggle close and tell each other jokes.

Rodrigo laughs in his sleep.

Tonight, they hope.

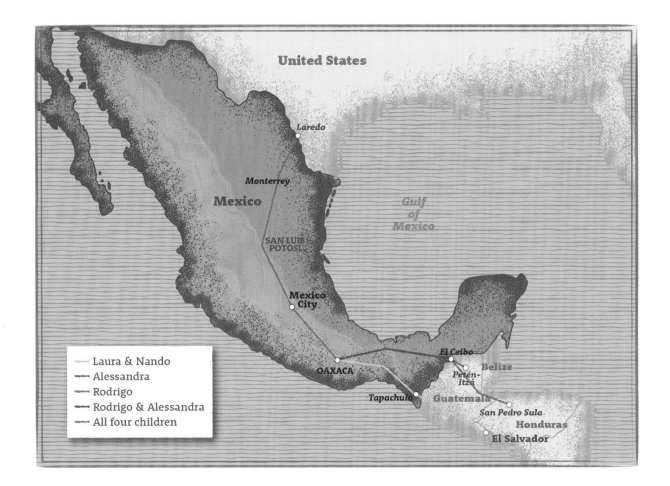

Legend:
- Laura & Nando
- Alessandra
- Rodrigo
- Rodrigo & Alessandra
- All four children

A Note from Baylor University

While the characters in this book are composites, their stories are real. Most children migrate to reunite with family members in the United States, and most migrants flee some form of violence. Central America's notorious street gangs recruit children as young as eight and force them to join. Many children, like Rodrigo, believe the authorities cannot be trusted to keep them safe; their only option is to leave. Alessandra, like many Mayan children, is especially vulnerable because of her indigenous heritage. She will have difficulty communicating with the other children she meets on the journey because she speaks the Mayan language Q'eqchi' and not Spanish.

The journey from the Guatemalan border through Mexico to the U.S. is long and arduous. From the Suchiate River, where Laura and Nando enter Mexico, it is more than 1,000 miles to Nuevo Laredo and almost twice as far to San Diego. The notorious network of trains known as La Bestia, or "the Beast," is the most dangerous part of the journey. As the book's illustrations depict, this is never the only way migrants travel. They use a combination of walking, taking public transportation, and riding in the back of large cargo trucks.

While the pathway through Mexico is very dangerous, and migrants are regularly victimized along the way, many also experience great kindness. A network of shelters exists throughout the country, and many individuals and organizations actively work to help by providing food, shelter, clothing, medical care, legal services, and more.

Our story ends with the children looking across the border hoping for a better, safer future. Tomorrow, they will present themselves to immigration officials and request asylum. Here, the long and difficult journey through the U.S. immigration system begins.

Children are initially held in Customs and Border Patrol (CBP) facilities and by law must be transferred to a shelter or foster home run by the Office of Refugee Resettlement (ORR) within 72 hours, though it is common for children to be held by CBP for several days or even weeks.

Children typically spend about two months in the ORR facilities, where they are required to receive education and health services as they await placement with a family member or sponsor. Once released to a sponsor, the children petition for asylum or another form of relief within the immigration court system. These cases can take anywhere from six months to two years, and, if successful, the children will be allowed to stay in the U.S.

Once children are in the U.S., either awaiting a court date or after a successful asylum hearing, their journey is far from over. They need to learn how to live in a new country, with a new language, at a new school, with relatives whom they often haven't seen in years and may hardly know.

How to Get Involved

Organizations across the U.S. are working to address the needs of children like Alessandra, Nando, Laura, and Rodrigo by providing them with safe places, legal services, education, and health care. Initially, children seeking asylum need help finding and paying for lawyers because their cases are civil matters, not criminal, which means that they have a right to an attorney but are not provided with one. Many groups exist to provide these services to unaccompanied minors, but they are understaffed, underfunded, and overwhelmed by their case load. Various resettlement groups and nonprofits help the children enroll in schools, learn English, and connect to tutors in their area as they adjust to life in the U.S. While children receive medical attention within the immigration system, they require ongoing health services for their physical and mental well-being.

These migrant children have experienced untold horrors—the trauma that forced them to leave their home countries, the violence and hardships they experienced along the way, and the difficulties of adapting to a new place, culture, and family. Counselors, social service providers, and faith-based groups in communities across the country are helping these children recover from trauma and restore their health. We encourage you to help by volunteering and partnering with organizations in your community.

The Global Hunger and Migration Project

In 2017, Baylor University launched a series of projects to create teams of students and professors to conduct research and design interventions that address some of the world's most complex issues. Drs. Lori Baker and Victor Hinojosa launched the project that is now the Global Hunger and Migration Project (GHMP) within Baylor's Collaborative on Hunger and Poverty. While the GHMP aims to expand its research and reach to countries around the globe, current teams within the GHMP focus on the migration crisis in Central America. Since 2014, more than 850,000 children and families have fled from Guatemala, El Salvador, and Honduras to the U.S. seeking asylum. More than 250,000 of these individuals are, like Rodrigo, Alessandra, Nando, and Laura, children and youth who made this journey alone.

At Baylor, we are committed to understanding this crisis in all of its complexity, including push factors that cause immigrants to leave their homes, the journey itself, and the reality of the immigration system in the U.S. We work to conduct research and design interventions at each of these points with the goal of integrating research, education, policy analysis, and community engagement to effect change in the spheres of hunger and migration across the world. Our projects are meant to foster understanding and engagement with this crisis in the classroom and beyond by equipping students and practitioners with skills and tools to identify promising practices to address these issues. This book is an example of one project that tells refugee children's stories with the hope that we will better understand their journey so that we can make the best informed response to this problem.

Acknowledgments

This book, published in partnership between Baylor University and Six Foot Press, is the result of research conducted by Baylor undergraduate students as part of the GHMP in a course called "Child Migration in the Western Hemisphere." This course utilizes design thinking techniques to teach students that they can engage with the world's greatest and most daunting problems. Over the course of four semesters, the following students designed this project, conducted its research, and drafted our characters' storyline and route: Maddy Abdallah, Adele Allen, Caroline Capili, Julia Castillo, Corrie Coleman, Savannah Cone, Alexia Contreras, Rachel Cummins, Bailey Craig, Claire Crites, Kendall Curtis, Juni Darling, Mishell Espinoza, Bethany Fernandes, Katie Frost, Chris Gonzalez, Jeshua Gonzalez, Ashlin Gray, Carolina Gutierrez, Abigail Haan, Abby Harris, Catherine Haseman, Holly Herald, Susan Herrera, Aime Hogue, Lorena Martinez, Austin McDaniel, Shannon McKim, Damian Moncada, Hannah Neel, Dalilah Negrete, Alex Oh, Ana O'Quin, Annie Richmond, Katie Rivera, Kristopher Ruiz, Bonnie Ryan, Camille Rybacki, Lawson Sadler, Kylie Smith, Marianne Sullivan, Margaret Thonnard, Joshua Upham, Ben Valle, Emma Valle, Elizabeth Velasquez, Rebecca Voth, Jeffrey Wang, Natalie Widdows, and Ashley Yeaman.

We offer special thanks to Lori Baker, Andy Hogue, Kingsley East, Andrew Patterson, and everyone at Baylor University who worked to make this project possible, as well as the team at Six Foot Press.